FLEX

Connect, Empower, & Lead

A Teen's Guide to Leadership

BY SHAINE HOBDY

TABLE OF CONTENTS

ABOUT
SHAINE HOBDY

About Shaine Hobdy

Shaine Hobdy is a leadership coach, award winning author, and curriculum designer who builds practical, people-first tools that help emerging leaders grow with confidence. He is the author of **"Coach To ALIGN: Building Empowered Teams Together"**, which won two International Impact Book Awards for leadership, and he brings that same evidence-informed clarity to this book.

Shaine wrote **"FLEX: Connect. Empower. Lead - A Teen's Guide to Leadership"** from decades of developing new leaders across organizations, with the singular purpose of making leadership accessible, actionable, and rooted in real-world practice.

He is passionate about teaching young people how to identify personality styles, flex their approach to different people and situations, and build the communication and decision-making skills that shape long-term success. Shaine combines storytelling, experiential exercises, and simple frameworks so teens can practice leadership today and lead with integrity tomorrow.

Shaine has spent over four decades helping people work better together. From leading high-performing teams to training frontline employees, Shaine has built a career around one core belief: **when people feel seen, supported, and understood, they do their best work**.

His leadership journey spans operations, training, customer service, and organizational development. Whether coaching new leaders, guiding seasoned professionals, or helping teams rebuild trust, Shaine brings a grounded, practical approach rooted in real-world experience.

Over the years, he has facilitated workshops, coached executives, and developed employee programs used across multiple industries. His **ALIGN Coaching Model** and **FLEX** communication framework have been shared with leaders, educators, and teams looking to strengthen relationships and drive meaningful results.

Shaine's work continues to inspire a new generation of leaders — **one conversation, one connection, one FLEX at a time.**

The Mission & The Heart Behind FLEX

At the center of Shaine's work is a mission: **to help people communicate with confidence, compassion, and clarity — no matter their personality or background.**

Shaine believes leadership isn't about titles or authority; it's about connection. It's about how you show up, how you listen, and how you treat people in every interaction. **FLEX** was born from years of watching teams struggle not because of skill gaps, but because of **communication gaps**.

Shaine created **FLEX** to give teens a simple, powerful way to understand themselves and others. He wanted a tool that made communication feel easy — something relatable, memorable, and usable in real-life moments like group projects, friendships, sports teams, and family conversations.

Every chapter in this book reflects Shaine's belief: **When you understand people, you can connect with people. And, when you can connect, you can lead.**

★ BOOK OVERVIEW

This book helps teens discover how to flex their personalities—not to fake who they are, but to connect, communicate, and empower others.

Through stories, exercises, and "Coach's Corner" tips, readers learn how to recognize the four personality types, adapt to others, and create stronger relationships—in school, sports, friendships, and family life.

LEARNING GOALS

- Recognize their own dominant style (Feeler, Controller, Thinker, or Entertainer.).

- Understand how different styles communicate and make decisions.

- Flex their approach to reduce conflict and increase connection.

- Empower others through empathy, curiosity, and teamwork.

Dedication

For my friends and family —
thank you for your steady belief, honest feedback, and the quiet sacrifices that make every step forward possible.

For my team — The Shaine Train
this book is for the daily effort you bring, the care you show our customers, and the courage you take in doing the work right. I strive to lead by example so each of you feels proud of your job, your impact, and the company we build together.

For the young people who inspire me—
your curiosity, courage, and care remind me why leadership matters. You push me to be better every day, and this guide is written to help you step into that power with clarity and heart.

Shaine Hobdy

F – Find your style

Know who you are.
Know your strengths.
Know your tendencies.

L – Learn about others

Stay curious. Notice
how people think,
speak, and react.

E – Empathize

See the world from
someone else's shoes –

X – eXpand your impact

Make a difference –
and help people thrive.

F = FIND YOUR STYLE

Knowing your style helps you show up as yourself. Find your style means noticing what you enjoy, how you like to speak and work, and what makes you feel confident. When you know this, you make choices that match who you are and others can trust and follow you. Flexing starts with being clear about your own strengths.

L = LEARN ABOUT OTHERS

Leaders pay attention to people different from them. Learn about others means watching how friends, teammates, and classmates think, communicate, and solve problems. The more you understand other styles, the better you can include them, avoid misunderstandings, and get more done together. Learning others' ways makes your team stronger.

E = EMPATHIZE

Empathy is the bridge between people. Empathize means trying to feel what someone else feels and saying it back so they know you get them.

When you empathize, you calm conflicts, build trust, and help people do their best. Flexing your personality to match emotional needs makes you a safer and more effective leader.

X = EXPAND YOUR IMPACT

Expanding your impact is using what you know to help more people. Expand your impact means mixing your style with what you've learned about others and using empathy to bring everyone along.

When you *flex*—adapting your words, tone, or actions—you connect with more people and make bigger change. That's how small choices turn into real leadership.

FLEXING vs. FAKING

Why flex your personality, not fake it

- **Build real trust –** People sense when you're genuine; flexing shows you're adapting, faking feels dishonest.

- **Keep your energy –** Flexing uses your strengths; faking drains you and burns out your confidence.

- **Grow for real –** Flexing helps you learn new skills; faking only hides gaps and stops improvement.

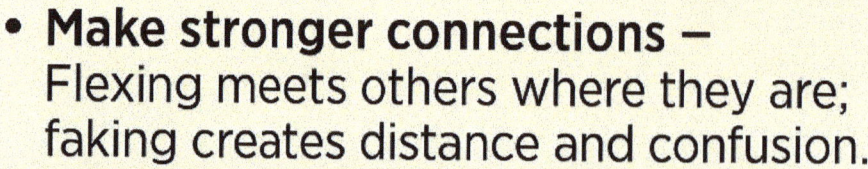

- **Make stronger connections –** Flexing meets others where they are; faking creates distance and confusion.

- **Lead with respect –** Flexing earns respect because it's intentional; faking risks losing credibility.

Connection = Empowerment

INTERACTIVE
REFLECTION

(FLEX)

Think and write below:

1 Think of a misunderstanding.
_____
_____
_____

2 Did you flex?
_____
_____
_____

3 How could you flex next time?
_____
_____
_____
_____
_____

JOURNAL NOTE PAGE

_____

_____

_____

_____

_____

_____

_____

_____

_____

_____

_____

_____

_____

_____

_____

_____

_____

CHAPTER 2
THE FOUR STYLES

The Feeler

Feelers lead with heart. They care deeply and build trust through empathy.

Meet Maya
– Feeler

Feelers care a lot about other people and focus on building strong friendships. They do best when others notice their help and when the team makes them feel safe and respected.

In a group, Feelers keep morale high and help everyone trust each other. They like feedback that is kind and encouraging, not harsh.

Leaders can support Feelers grow by giving supportive praise, showing how their work matters, and offering gentle tips to stretch their skills. This makes Feelers feel valued and ready to try new things.

The Thinker

Thinkers lead with reason. They love solving puzzles and making smart choices.

Meet Sam – Thinker

Thinkers like to use logic and facts to solve problems. They pay attention to details, follow steps, and feel most comfortable when instructions are clear and organized.

In a group, Thinkers help the team make smart, well-planned decisions by spotting patterns and checking the facts. They prefer feedback that is specific and based on results, not just feelings.

Leaders can support Thinkers by giving clear, detailed guidance, showing data or examples, and offering concrete steps for improvement. This helps Thinkers stay confident and keep getting better.

THE CONTROLLER

Controllers lead with direction. They take charge and make sure the team stays on track.

Meet Jordan - Controller

Controllers are decisive, get-things-done team members who like clear goals and fast action. They feel motivated when tasks, deadlines, and responsibilities are obvious.

In a group, Controllers push the team forward by keeping projects on track and making quick decisions when needed. They help turn ideas into results and expect everyone to follow the plan.

Leaders can support Controllers by giving direct, specific feedback focused on what to change and why. Clear steps, measurable targets, and accountability let Controllers use their drive for efficiency to deliver concrete results.

Meet Aiden – Entertainer

Entertainers bring energy, creativity, and fresh ideas to a team. They make work fun, spark new ways to solve problems, and often inspire others with their enthusiasm.

They do best when leaders notice their creativity and give them room to try new things, but also show how those ideas link to the team's goals. Feedback that mixes encouragement with a few clear next steps helps Entertainers turn inspiration into results.

Leaders can get the most from Entertainers by recognizing their strengths, asking them to focus their ideas around a goal, and offering short, actionable guidance so their energy leads to real progress.

"Great leaders learn to flex — adjusting their approach to connect with others."

JOURNAL NOTE PAGE

None of these are wrong. None of them are better. They're just different ways of moving through the world.

When you understand these differences, the tension drops—and teamwork finally makes sense.

Clashes happen when someone expects the world to think and communicate exactly the way they do. But in reality...

FLEX FIX GRID

FEELER + CONTROLLER	THINKER ENTERTAINER	CONTROLLER + THINKER
COMMON CLASH	**COMMON CLASH**	**COMMON CLASH**
Feelings vs. Efficiency	Logic vs. Excitement	Speed vs. Precision
WHY IT HAPPENS	**WHY IT HAPPENS**	**WHY IT HAPPENS**
Feeler wants harmony. Controller done.	Thinker wants facts. Entertainer wants fun.	Controller rushes. Thinker slows down to check details.
FLEX	**FLEX**	**FLEX**
"Let's get this done, but let's make sure everyone feels heard."	"Let's try your idea — but let's plan it step-by-step."	"Do we want quick or do we want perfect?"

reFLEXion
QUICK ~~REFLECTION~~

- **Which clash pair sounds MOST like you and your friends?**

_____

_____

_____

- **Which FLEX tip could you try this week?**

_____

_____

_____

- **Who do you understand a little better now?**

_____

_____

_____

JOURNAL NOTE PAGE

CHAPTER 4–
THE FLEX SKILL

Flexing helps you communicate with anyone, anywhere.

 # TALKING TO A FEELER?

- Be kind.
- Be warm. Show appreciation.

They hear your heart before they hear your words.

Try saying:

Thanks for your help — it really means a lot.

Talking to an Entertainer?

- Bring energy, creativity, and excitement.
- They connect to fun.

Try saying:

What if we tried something a little more exciting?

Talking to a Thinker?

- Give facts, details, and logical steps.
- They listen with their brain first.

Try saying:

Here's the data that explains why this works.

Talking to a Controller?

- Get to the point
- Keep it simple

They respect speed and clarity.

Try saying:

The fastest solution is this...

WHY FLEX WORKS

Think of FLEX as a superpower that makes communication click.

- It reduces misunderstandings.

- It helps ideas land better.

- It builds trust across totally different personalities.

- And it turns stress into teamwork — fast.

Practice Activity:
SAY IT 4 WAYS

Pick one sentence. Any sentence.
Now FLEX it four different ways.
Let's try the sentence:

"We need to finish this project today."

 For a Feeler

It'd mean a lot if
we could finish
this project today.

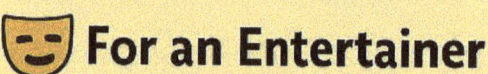

 **For a Thinker**

The data shows
we should finish this
project today.

😌 **For an Entertainer**

How fun would it be
to finish this project
today?

 **For a Controller**

Let's just finish this
project today.

FEELER VERSION

- Use empathy and compassion.
- Be considerate of others' feelings.
- Show support.
- Try saying:

Hey team, I appreciate everything you've done – can we wrap it up today so no one feels rushed tomorrow?

CONTROLLER VERSION

- **Get to the point. Keep it simple. Be confident.**

- **They respect speed and clarity.**

- **Try saying:**

We're finishing this today. Let's go.

ENTERTAINER VERSION

- **Bring energy, creativity, and excitement.**
- **They connect to fun.**
- **Try saying:**

JOURNAL NOTE PAGE

CHAPTER 5 IS ABOUT REAL-LIFE MOMENTS — THE ONES YOU ACTUALLY DEAL WITH AT SCHOOL:

GROUP PROJECTS.

SPORTS TEAMS.

TEXTS THAT GET TAKEN THE WRONG WAY.

DRAMA THAT EXPLODES OUT OF NOWHERE.

HERE'S THE GOOD NEWS:

When things get messy, FLEX makes them manageable.
Let's jump into the three biggest school situations where FLEX turns chaos into connection.

Everyone wants something different.

Everyone's right... but no one's connecting.

This is the moment where FLEX shines.

HOW TO FLEX IN GROUP PROJECTS

- **To the Feeler: Offer reassurance.**

  "Maya, thanks for making sure everyone's heard. Let's get everyone's ideas on the table first."

HOW TO FLEX IN GROUP PROJECTS

- **To the Controller: Give clarity.**

"Jordan, can you outline the steps you think we should take?"

HOW TO FLEX IN GROUP PROJECTS

- **To the Thinker: Bring structure.**
  "Sam, can you check the instructions to make sure we don't miss anything?"

HOW TO FLEX IN GROUP PROJECTS

- **To the Entertainer:** Add creativity after the plan is set.

> Aiden, once we have the outline. I want to hear your fun ideas.

Then the dots bubble… and disappear.

We've all been there. Tone is tricky – especially in text messages, where you don't hear voice or see facial expression.

HOW TO FLEX IN TEXTING

Think of each style before hitting send:

- **Feeler: Add warmth.**

Hey, no stress, just wondering – why'd you do that?

HOW TO FLEX IN TEXTING

Think of each style before hitting send:

- **Thinker: Be clear.**

Trying to understand the reason behind it – can you explain?

HOW TO FLEX IN TEXTING

Think of each style before hitting send:

- **Entertainer:** Soften with energy.

Lol wait, what made you do that?

ACTIVITY: THE FLEX CHALLENGE

Now it's your turn.

Here are three everyday messages. Rewrite each one four different ways, one for each style.

Be creative. Be honest. Be FLEX-y.

THE FLEX CHALLENGE

1. "Can we talk later?"

FEELER	THINKER
_____ _____ _____	_____ _____ _____

CONTROLLER	ENTERTAINER
_____ _____ _____	_____ _____ _____

THE FLEX CHALLENGE

2. "Please stop interrupting me."

FEELER	THINKER
_____	_____
_____	_____
_____	_____

CONTROLLER	ENTERTAINER
_____	_____
_____	_____
_____	_____

THE FLEX CHALLENGE

3. "I don't understand this assignment."

FEELER

_____
_____
_____

THINKER

_____
_____
_____

CONTROLLER

_____
_____

ENTERTAINER

_____
_____

When you FLEX:
- you reduce arguments,
- you increase understanding,
- you make every group you're in run smoother,
- and you become the teammate everyone wants.

School becomes easier — not because it is easier, but because you've become stronger at connecting.

JOURNAL NOTE PAGE

CHAPTER 6
FLEX FOR FRIENDSHIP & FAMILY

WHY FLEX MATTERS IN YOUR PERSONAL LIFE.

Friends. Siblings. Parents. People online.

They all communicate differently – and sometimes those differences feel HUGE.

PARENT (THINKER)

- Needs structure
- Wants tasks done when promised
- Believes "cleaning first = relaxing later"

AIDEN (ENTERTAINER)

- Works best with freedom
- Wants fun and flexibility
- Believes "chill first = inspiration later"

HOW TO RESPOND:

If they're a FEELER:

If they're a CONTROLLER:

Example 2 – THE SIBLING SHOWDOWN

Your sibling barges into your room without knocking (again).
Instead of screaming into the *void* – here's **how to FLEX your response:**

Here's how to FLEX your response:

To a FEELER sibling:

To a THINKER sibling:

Here's how to FLEX your response:

RELATIONSHIPS RUN ON FLEX

Think about the people you care about most. Each one has a different way of thinking, talking, and showing love.

FLEX helps you:

- avoid unnecessary fights
- apologize more meaningfully
- understand what people really mean
- express yourself in a way they can hear

One FLEX move at a time — that's how relationships grow.

REFLECTION PROMPT

Take a deep breath and ask yourself:

WHO IN YOUR LIFE DO YOU WANT TO UNDERSTAND BETTER?

- A parent?
- A friend you've been drifting from?
- A brother or sister who gets on your nerves?
- Someone you admire but find confusing?

Write their name. _____

Picture their vibe. _____

Guess their FLEX style. _____

_____

_____

UNDERSTANDING IS THE FIRST STEP TOWARD CONNECTION.

JOURNAL PROMPT

"How can I FLEX with them this week?"

- Think small.
- Think specific.
- Think real.

Here are examples:

- I'll give my Feeler friend extra reassurance.

- I'll keep my text short and clear for my Controller coach.

- I'll explain my reasoning better for my Thinker parent.

- I'll add some energy when talking to my Entertainer sibling.

JOURNAL NOTE PAGE

WHAT EMPOWERMENT REALLY MEANS

Some people think leadership means being the loudest voice in the room.

Or taking control.

Or making decisions for everyone.

But real leadership?

It's about bringing out the best in the people around you.

Great leaders don't say, "Everyone be like me."

They say,
"Let me understand you —
so you can shine in your
own way."

That's empowerment.

And FLEX is the key to unlocking it.

WHY FLEX = EMPOWERMENT

When you FLEX, you're paying attention to what others need:

THE ENTERTAINER
– THE SPARK

Entertainers energize people, spark creativity, and boost the mood. They bring joy to the grind.

How Entertainers Empower:

- They make the team feel excited
- They help brainstorm new ideas
- They encourage others to take risks
- They make hard tasks feel fun

Their superpower:

→ Inspiring energy

THE THINKER
– THE ARCHITECT

Thinkers bring logic, clarity, and structure.
They see details others miss.

How Thinkers Empower:

- They design systems that work
- They double-check instructions so nothing breaks
- They help teams make decisions based on facts
- They calm chaos with clear planning

Their superpower:

→ Designing systems

THE CONTROLLER
– THE PACE-SETTER

Controllers bring confidence, direction, and momentum. They don't just talk — they take action.

How Controllers Empower:

- They set clear goals
- They keep everyone on schedule
- They push teams to finish strong
- They jump in when something needs to get done

Their superpower:

→ Driving results

GROUP ACTIVITY: THE FLEX TEAM

Imagine you're building your dream team for a mission: Plan the ultimate school event.

Your job is to decide:

1. What is their role?

2. How do they help the team?

3. What happens if they're missing?

WHAT HAPPENS IF THEY ARE MISSING:

♥ THE FEELER – COMMUNITY BUILDER

Role: Making sure everyone feels included

Strength: Remembers who needs encouragement

What happens if they're missing:

• People feel ignored or discouraged

What happens if they're missing:

🎭 Entertainer – Hype Leader

- Role: Boosting energy and creativity
- Strength: Makes it fun

What happens if they're missing:

- Team feels bored or disconnected

TRY THESE FLEX MOVES THIS WEEK:

- **Ask a Feeler:** "What do you think would make everyone feel included?"

- **Ask a Controller:** "Can you help us stay on track?"

- **Ask a Thinker:** "Can you check if this makes sense?"

- **Ask an Entertainer:** "What's a more fun way to do this?"

JOURNAL NOTE PAGE

CHAPTER 8
THE FLEX LIFE

NOW IT'S TIME TO ZOOM OUT AND SEE THE BIGGER TRUTH:

Flexing isn't something you do once.

It's something you carry with you for life.

The **FLEX Life** means showing up with self-awareness, kindness, confidence, and connection — wherever you go.

The FLEX Formula—

Before you step into the world with your new superpower, let's recap the formula that started it all:

F – Find your style

Know who you are.
Know your strengths.
Know your tendencies.

L – Learn about others

Stay curious. Notice how people think, speak, and react.

E – Empathize

See the world from someone else's shoes –

X – eXpand your impact

Make a difference – and help people thrive.

REFLECTION EXERCISE

WHO HAVE YOU EMPOWERED THIS MONTH?

Close your eyes and think back through the last few weeks:

- Who did you encourage? _____

- Who did you listen to? _____

- Who did you help to feel understood?
  _____

- Who became more confident because of YOU? _____

- Who communicated better because you FLEXed? _____

_____

_____

_____

Maybe it was a friend who needed reassurance.

Maybe it was a sibling who needed patience.

Maybe it was a classmate who needed clarity.

Maybe it was you — giving yourself a moment to breathe.

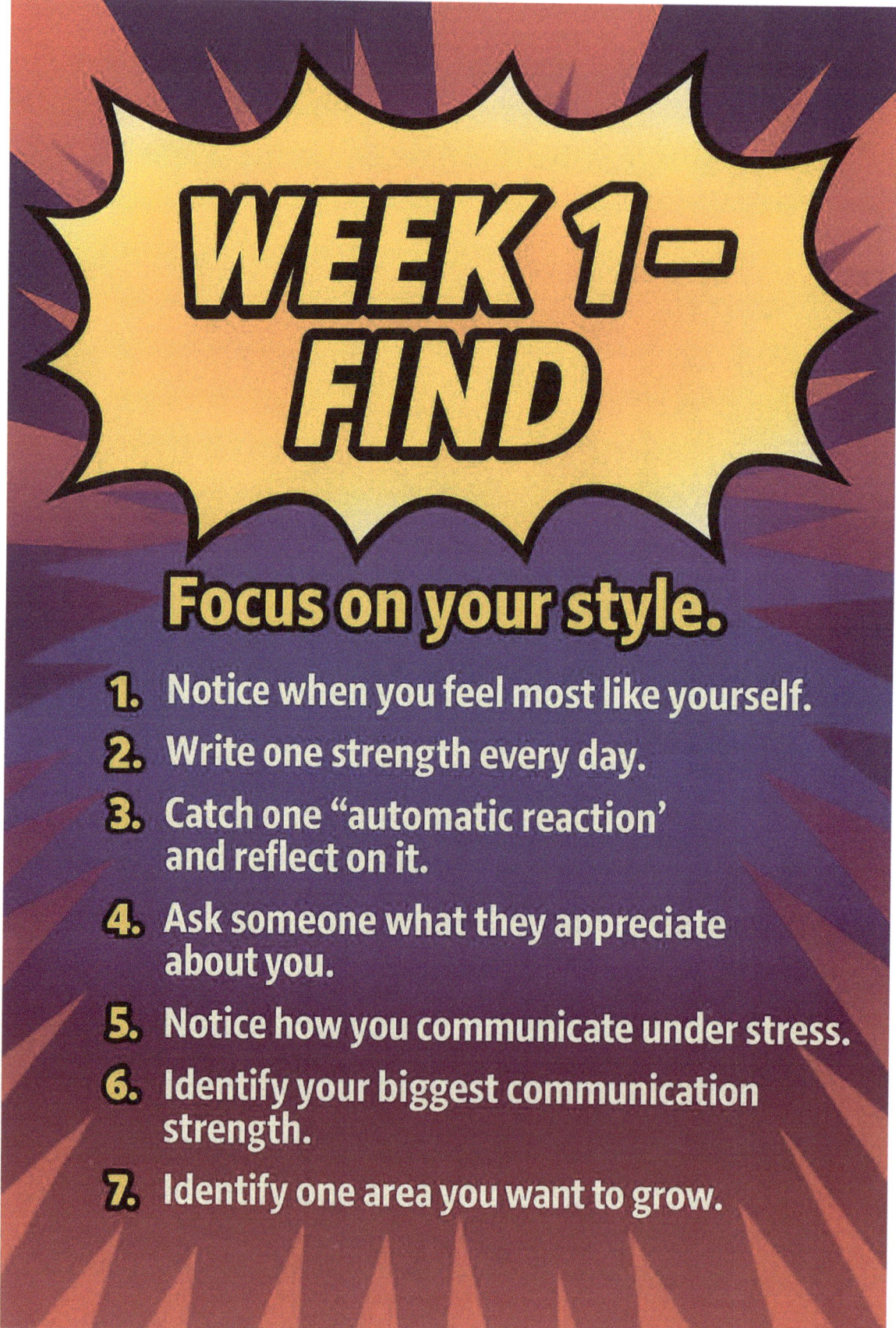

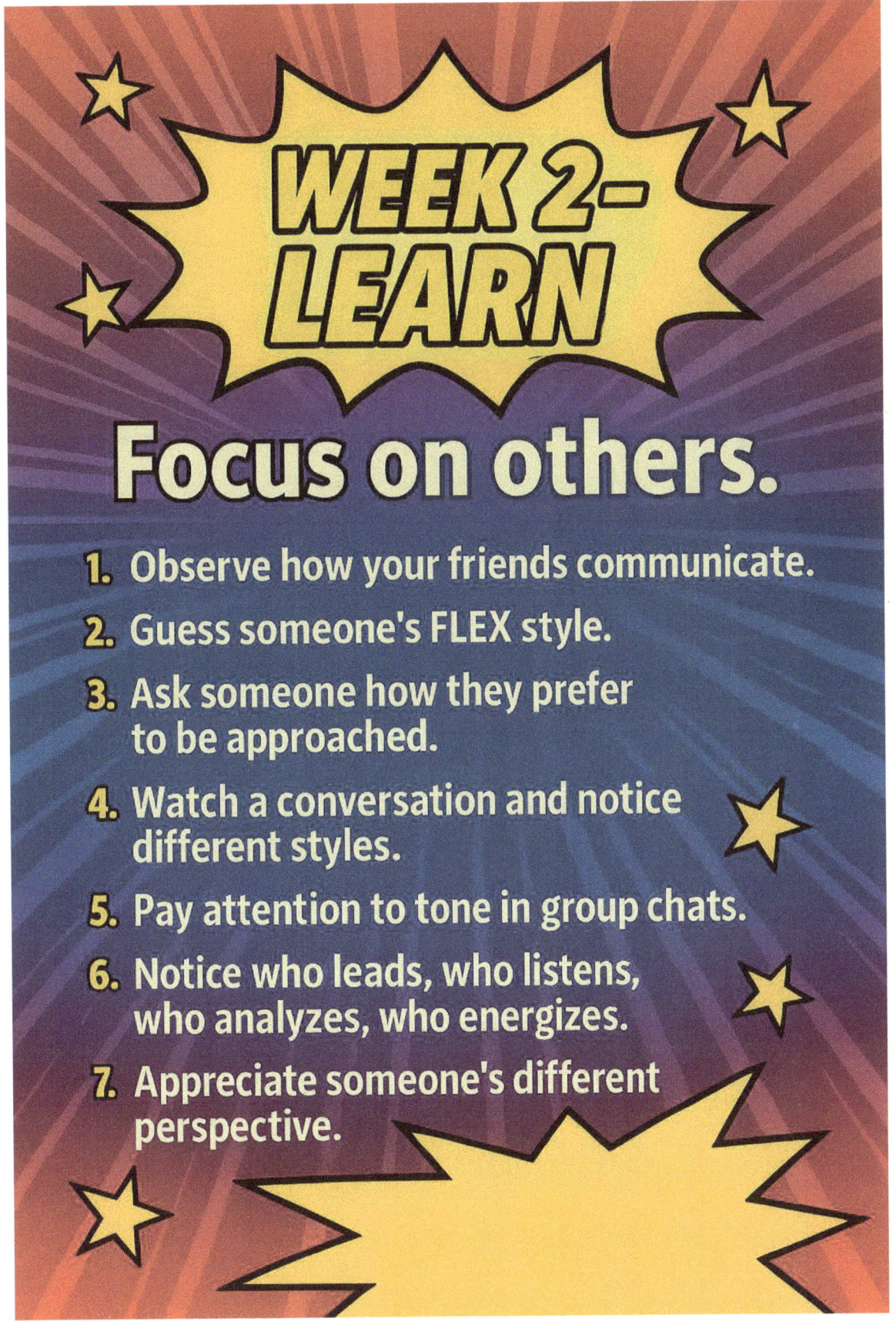

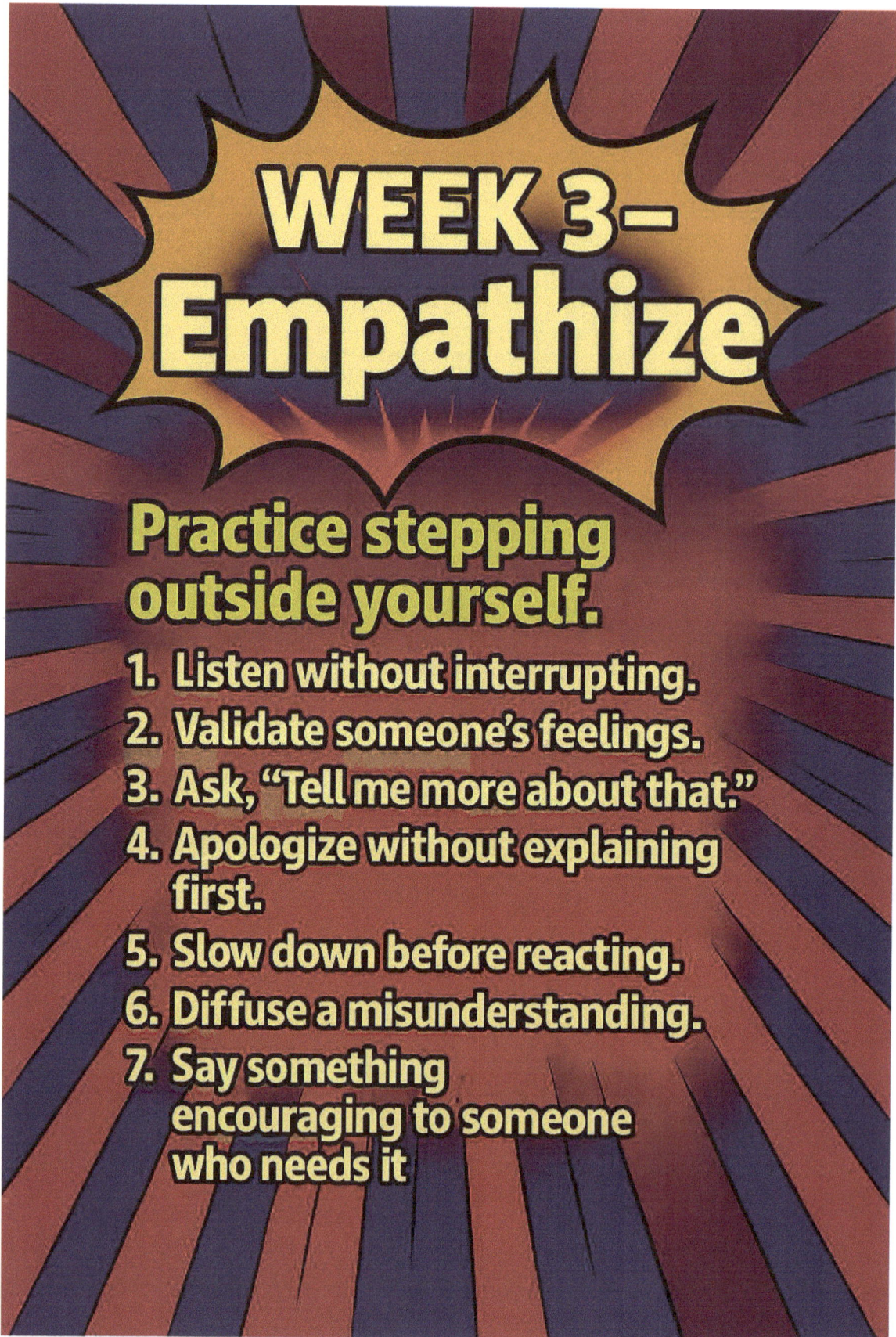

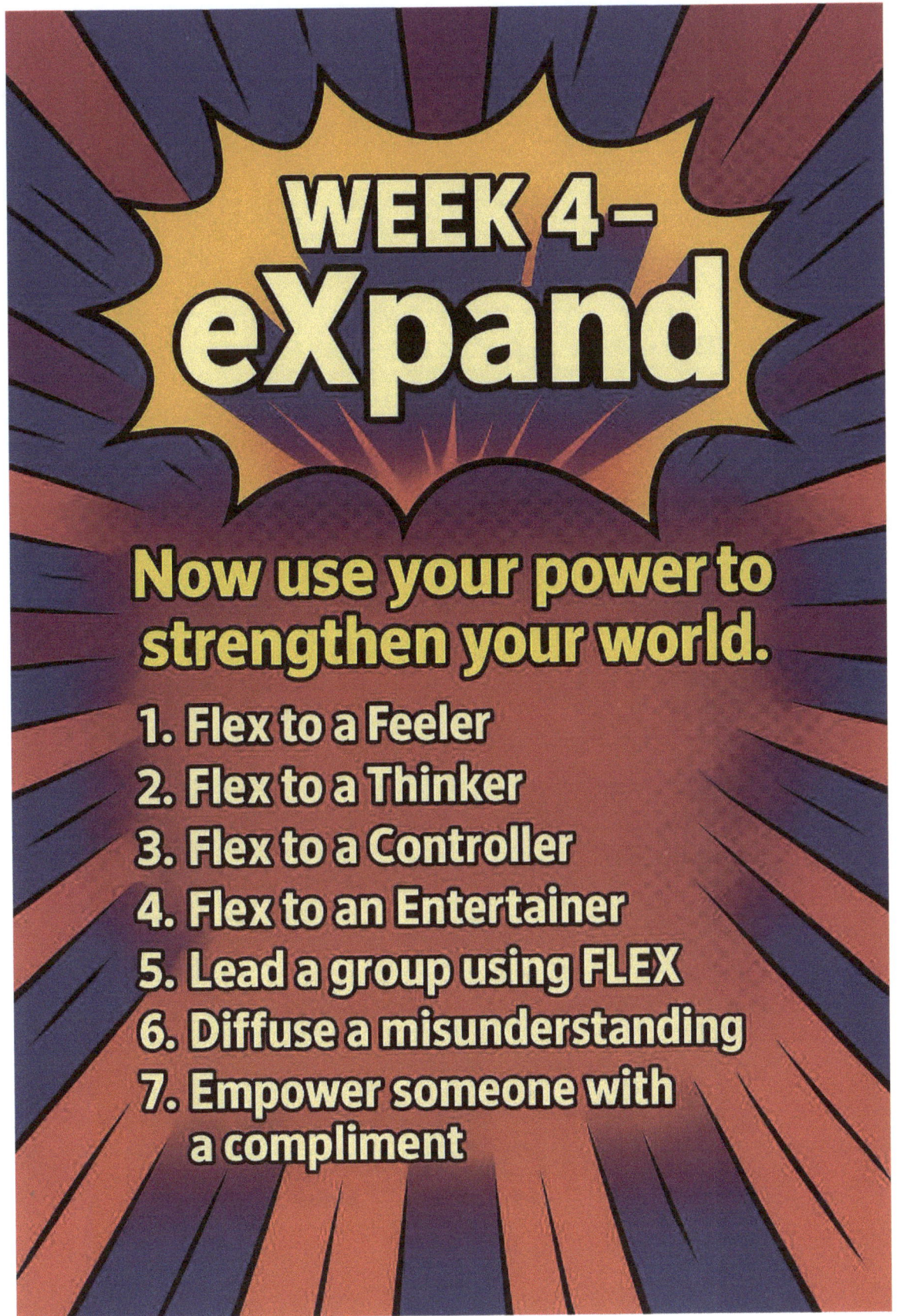

JOURNAL NOTE PAGE

JOURNAL NOTE PAGE

JOURNAL NOTE PAGE

TEEN
LEADERS
WANTED